Leopard Gecko Care

The Complete Guide to Caring for and Keeping Leopard Geckos as Pets

Tabitha Jones

Copyright © 2019 Tabitha Jones

All rights reserved.

Although the author and publisher have made every effort to ensure that the information presented in this book was correct at the present time, the author and publisher do not assume and hereby disclaim any liability to any party for any loss, damage, or disruption caused by errors or omissions, whether such errors or omissions result from negligence, accident, or any other cause.

ISBN: 9781799035282

CONTENTS

Introduction 6

Description 7

    Size 7

    Differences between the Sexes 7

    Natural habitat 8

    Behavior 8

    Crepuscular 8

    Diet 9

    Lifespan 9

    Teeth 9

Leopard Geckos as Pets 10

    Leopard Gecko Availability 10

    Selecting a Leopard Gecko For Purchase 10

    Handling 11

    Recording 11

Transporting your leopard gecko 12

    Container 12

- Heat 12
- Water 13

Housing your gecko 14

- Vivarium Specification 14
- Can Multiple Leopard Geckos be Housed Together? 14
- Hides and Shelter 15

Substrates 16

- Best Practice 16
- Substrate to Avoid 16

Heating and Lighting 17

- Heating 17
- Lighting 18

Feeding and Watering Your Pet 19

- What do Leopard Geckos Eat? 19
- Pros and Cons of Crickets 19
- Pros and Cons of Mealworms 20
- Are Mealworms Dangerous for Geckos? 21
- Gut Loading 21
- Dusting the Prey 21

- Pinkies and Waxworms 22
- How much do Geckos eat? 22
- Watering 23

Shedding 24
- How to tell if your Gecko is about to Shed 24
- Is it normal for my Gecko to eat its shed skin? 24
- A Moist Shelter 25

Breeding 26
- How to tell if a Female Gecko is Pregnant 26
- Eggs 26

Hibernation 27
- How to Hibernate your Gecko 27

Final Thoughts 28

ABOUT THE AUTHOR 30

INTRODUCTION

The leopard gecko (scientifically known as *Eublepharis macularius*) is a crepuscular ground-dwelling lizard. Unlike the majority of other gecko species, the leopard gecko possesses moveable eyelids which gives the gecko an anthropomorphic quality. The specie's extraordinary set of eyelids is the basis for the scientific name. *Eublepharis* is a combination of the Greek words *Eu*, meaning 'good,' and *Blephar*, meaning 'eyelid.' The name *Macularius* is derived from the Latin word *Macula* which translates to 'spot' or 'blemish' which is in obvious reference to the animal's spotted markings. They are naturally found in the deserts of Asia, Pakistan and northern India.

DESCRIPTION

Leopard geckos have become a very popular, and common, pet and have been extensively bred within the United States over the last thirty years. Due to the extensive breeding there are multiple different colour morphs available which adds to the desirability of the leopard gecko as a pet.

Size

Leopard geckos are among the largest of all gecko subspecies. Hatchlings tend to be between 2.6 to 3.3 inches (or 6.5 to 8.5cm) in size and a hatchling's weight is normally around 3 grams. Adult leopard geckos are normally 8.1 to 11 inches (or 20.5 to 27.5cm) and their weight is normally between 45 to 65 grams depending on their size.

Differences between the Sexes

There is little sexual dimorphism between male and female leopard geckos and it is almost impossible to judge the sex of a leopard gecko at first glance. In general males have larger and broader bodies and heads than females – however due to the extensive breeding of the leopard gecko this is not the best practice in determining a gecko's sex. Only by checking the underside of a gecko can its sex be determined. Males have a V-shaped set of pre-anal pores and hemipenal bulges while females have smaller pores and do not have an external hemipenal bulge.

Natural habitat

In the wild the leopard gecko is most at home in rocky environments, dry grasslands and desert regions. As previously mentioned they are commonly found in the deserts of Asia, Pakistan and northern India. Due to their location the leopard gecko is able to survive in both warm and cold climates. During the winter, and cold months, they hibernate underground and live of the fat supplies stored within their tails.

Behavior

Due to the fact that they have been such popular pets for a long period of time, the leopard gecko is considered to be the first domesticated lizard species. They have a docile temperament and are relatively easy to care for which makes them the perfect pet for beginner lizard keepers. Leopard geckos are normally solitary and do not tend to live with other animals.

Crepuscular

The leopard gecko is a crepuscular lizard. For an animal to be classified as crepuscular they have to be primarily active during twilight (the period before dawn and the period after dusk). Crepuscular animals are not the same as nocturnal animals. Crepuscular animals may also become active during nights with bright moonlight or on dark overcast days. It is important to take the leopard geckos crepuscular nature into account when choosing a place to house your lizard.

Diet

Leopard geckos in the wild mainly feed on crickets, cockroaches, grasshoppers, spiders, moths, ants, different types of worms and other similar small insects. They have an incredibly keen sense of sight and smell which allows them to efficiently stalk their prey in the wild.

Lifespan

Leopard geckos are relatively long living in comparison to other reptiles. On average leopard geckos live for around 10 years. Males normally live longer than females do and it is not uncommon for them to live for close to 20 years. The oldest recorded leopard gecko is 27½ years old and still breeding!

Teeth

Leopard geckos are polyphyodont which means that they are able to replace each one of their 100 teeth every 3 to 4 months. Next to each fully formed adult tooth there is a small replacement tooth developing from a stem cell in the dental lamina (a band of tissue surrounding the tooth).

LEOPARD GECKOS AS PETS

Leopard geckos have become one of the most popular reptile pets. As previously mentioned they are docile and considered the only domesticated lizard species. Due to the ease of breeding leopard geckos, the majority that are sold as pets have been captive-bred rather than wild-caught.

Leopard Gecko Availability

There are multiple different methods available to a potential pet own when it comes to actually purchasing their gecko. The most common of these methods of purchase are as follows: pet stores, reptile shows, breeders and the internet. Many breeders and breeding websites give information about the specific morphs and health of geckos they have available. Most leopard geckos will be priced between $20 to $150. However due to the large collector market worldwide some rare variations of the leopard gecko have been known to sell for as much as $3000!

Selecting a Leopard Gecko For Purchase

When selecting your gecko for purchase it is always best practice to actually view the gecko in person to check for any obvious signs of ill health. The gecko should appear alert during your viewing. If possible it is best to try and see the gecko feed as this will give you a good idea of the gecko's eating habits and if it has any issues during feeding. It is best practice to purchase captively bred geckos rather than wild-caught geckos due to the wide availability of geckos bred in captivity and to therefore eliminate any chance of genetic problem.

Handling

If you want to handle your gecko on a regular basis it is best practice to start handling your gecko during its juvenile stage as it will normalize the handling process. However it is important to allow your gecko to explore its new home and become settled before attempting to handle it. You will know when your gecko has become settled in its vivarium when it leaves the hide. It is important to allow your gecko to get used to being in your hand. To maximize your geckos comfort it is important to not make any sudden movements while the gecko is being handled. Leopard geckos do not innately desire companionship and will therefore become more friendly and sociable the more you handle and play with them. When it comes to actually picking up your gecko the best practice is to place your hand into the vivarium and to allow the leopard gecko to approach your hand and eventually climb onto it. If it is imperative to pick up your gecko quickly, without waiting for it to crawl onto your hand on its own accord, it is best practice to pick the gecko up by its midsection and use as many fingers as possible to gain a sturdy but gentle grip on your gecko. While handling your lizard you should always have your free hand cupped underneath the hand holding the gecko as a preemptive precaution to catch the gecko if it falls.

Recording

It is highly advisable to keep a record throughout your geckos life. By regularly noting down weight, length and feeding patterns you will have a useful resource to help notice any potential problems with your gecko and to likewise make sure it is in good health.

TRANSPORTING YOUR LEOPARD GECKO

Whenever you purchase a new pet it is important to understand how to transport your pet from the location of purchase to your home safely without causing the pet any form of stress. Leopard geckos are reasonably hardy lizards and it is therefore very easy to transport them safely if the following steps are followed.

Container

A large see through Tupperware container is the most common manner of transporting newly purchased leopard geckos (it is also common for a cricket tub to be used if the gecko is small or still within its juvenile phase of development). It is important to make sure that whatever container you use to transport your gecko has a tightly sealing lid and is equipped with multiple air holes to allow for a decent air circulation. It is common practice to line the bottom of the container with a paper towel to cushion any potential knocks during the journey, provide a surface with grip for the gecko and to also clean the container easily. If it is possible you should try to include a hide from the gecko's vivarium to provide the gecko with a space it recognizes during the journey – this greatly reduces the chance of the lizard becoming stressed. It is important to not transport multiple geckos in the same container as the cramped conditions are likely to cause the lizards stress.

Heat

For short journeys (30mins or less) it is not essential to provide your gecko with a heat source during the journey as due to their hardy nature the short term drop in temperature will not affect the geckos health. For longer journeys it is best practice to have either a hot water bottle or a heat pack under your geckos container at all times during the journey as both should provide adequate heat levels during the transportation process. If you decide to use a hot water bottle as your heat source it is important to have hot water in a thermos to change the water when it gets cold. If you are using a battery powered heat pack it is likewise important to bring a spare change of batteries.

Water

It is important to provide water for your gecko during the transportation process if the journey is going to be more than a few hours long. Providing a water bowl within the geckos container can work but it is also likely to spill during the journey which can ruin the paper towel lining of the container. It is therefore best practice to provide your pet with water during the journey by, if possible, halting your transit to avoid spillage.

HOUSING YOUR GECKO

When looking to purchase a vivarium for your gecko it is important to remember that any vivarium designed for juvenile geckos will be outgrown quickly so it is advisable to purchase an adult-sized vivarium from the outset. This section will address the best practices for housing your gecko.

Vivarium Specification

The minimum size for a vivarium should be around the size of a 10-gallon aquarium. However your gecko will appreciate having a larger vivarium as it allows them to have more space to both explore and regulate their body temperature. An example of a larger vivarium size is a 30-gallon aquarium. The gecko's vivarium does not need to have a screen, or mesh, lid as the leopard gecko does not have toe pads – meaning that it is unable to climb the walls of the vivarium. However it is strongly recommended that you still purchase a vivarium with a lid if you will be housing your gecko in an environment which contains other house hold pets or small children. A lid to the vivarium also prevents crickets from being able to escape which is a bonus. It is important that the vivarium you choose to house your gecko in is easy to clean to avoid the buildup of bacteria.

Can Multiple Leopard Geckos be Housed Together?

Multiple leopard geckos can be house together in a single vivarium – as long as there is enough space for the geckos to live comfortably. Female geckos of a similar size can be housed together without any issues. Male geckos, on the other hand, need to be housed separately due to the fact that they are territorial and will tend to fight each other. It is possible to house multiple females and a single male together in the same vivarium without any issues. It is important that any geckos you house together are of a similar size to avoid a single gecko dominating the hides and food supply. If a drastic size difference develops it is advisable to separate the largest lizard from the smaller ones.

Hides and Shelter

To ensure that your leopard gecko feels comfortable and exhibits natural behavior it is important to provide your gecko with hiding places as well as sturdy rocks and branches for your gecko to explore. It is important to remember that leopard geckos are a nocturnal species and in the wild they remain hidden beneath rocks and other objects during the day light. For this reason it is also important to provide your gecko with a shelter for the day light hours. A shelter can be made out of household objects (such as a paper towel tube, a small cardboard box or a yoghurt pot) or purchased from pet stores and specialized reptile stores (such as ceramic caves, wooden shelters and caulk caves). Providing multiple shelters within the vivarium allows for the gecko to choose a hide that suits its current temperature requirement and mood.

SUBSTRATES

The term Substrate is defined as being the surface or material on which an organism lives, grows or obtains its nourishment. In terms of leopard gecko care the substrate is what you choose to line your gecko's vivarium. There are multiple different substrates available to use in your vivarium.

Best Practice

Juvenile geckos can be kept on paper towels or newspaper until they reach between 4 and 6 inches in length. Both paper towels and newspaper are widely availed, inexpensive and absorbent materials which help during the process of cleaning the vivarium. A vivarium of an adult gecko can be lined with sand to more closely recreate their natural habitat. If you are going to choose to use sand as your substrate of choice it is recommended to use 'Play Sand' due to the fact that it has been screened and washed which will lead to less chance of illness if your gecko happens to ingest it. It is best practice to use as fine a sand as possible when lining your vivarium as it minimizes the impact that any ingested sand will have on the geckos digestive track.

Substrate to Avoid

Sand should be avoided for juvenile geckos as they are likely to ingest it. Similarly calcium sands should be avoided due to the large size of the grains of the sand. It is also important to not use any commercial plant soils as they may contain fertilizer or pesticides which will have a negative impact on your geckos health.

HEATING AND LIGHTING

All species of reptile require a temperature gradient within their vivarium to allow them to select a temperature that best suits their individual needs at any given moment. It is important to optimize both temperature and lighting to create a comfortable habitat for your gecko.

Heating

It is important to place your method of heating on one side of your vivarium to allow for a natural temperature gradient to be created. It is best practice to use an under tank heater (such as the 'Zoo Med Repti Therm U.T.H'). Under tank heaters come in various sizes which allows you to choose the best one to create a temperature gradient within your vivarium. It is likewise important to have a decent thermometer available to check the temperature gradient within your vivarium. It is best practice to use a thermometer which is not fixed to the side of the vivarium. By attaching the thermometer to a wall of the vivarium you will only be measuring the temperature of the air within the tank rather and the temperature of the actual surfaces your gecko resides on. Hot rocks and heat stones are an alternative method of heating your geckos vivarium. Hot rocks and heat stones are not considered best practice for heating a reptile vivarium due to the fact that they can potentially become too hot which can lead to the reptile burning themselves. The ideal temperature for a leopard gecko vivarium is between 90 and 80 degrees Fahrenheit across the temperature gradient. Likewise it is best for the ambient air of the vivarium to be around 73 degrees Fahrenheit.

Lighting

Leopard geckos are a crepuscular species so no form of UV light is necessary within their vivarium. A simple low-wattage light can be placed on top of the cage and left on in 12 hour intervals to simulate natural lighting. It is important to not leave the light on for more than 12 hours a day due to the fact that too much exposure to light can cause your gecko to become stressed which can lead to a wide variety of health problems: ranging from the gecko refusing to eat to the death of the gecko. The main reason a light is used is to allow the owner to actually view their pet. It is possible to light your gecko cage 24/7 if you use a bulb which omits red light as it is invisible to leopard geckos which optimizes the viewing experience at no impact to the geckos light exposure.

FEEDING AND WATERING YOUR PET

Leopard geckos are relatively easy to provide for in terms of food and water which makes them an excellent pet for beginner lizard owners. The feeding process is made easier by the fact that their primary food sources are easily obtainable. However the following section will discuss, and explain, some important tips to help optimize the feeding process to keep your leopard gecko as healthy as possible.

What do Leopard Geckos Eat?

Leopard geckos do not eat plants or vegetables but will eat a wide variety of live prey including crickets, superworms, mealworms, and wax worms. It is also not uncommon for an adult leopard gecko to be fed pinkies (a pinkie is a baby mouse who is only a few days old). The two most common prey used to feed leopard geckos are crickets and mealworms – however which of these food choices is better?

Pros and Cons of Crickets

The main pros of using crickets as the your pets main food source is the fact that they are nutritionally superior to mealworms and are likewise more active prey which creates a more stimulating feeding process for your leopard gecko. However there are multiple downsides to using crickets as your primary prey choice. Buying crickets in bulk means that you will have to worry about looking after the crickets before using them as prey (which means providing them with food and water). Likewise it is important to note that any large amounts of crickets will produce a significant amount of noise due to their consistent chirping. Another potential negative of using crickets as your primary food choice is the fact that they can easily escape either from the gecko's vivarium or the cage you are keeping the crickets in before they are used as prey. Lastly it is also possible for uneaten crickets to eat your gecko's fecal matter, which will contain harmful parasites, which will then be transferred to your gecko during the feeding process.

Pros and Cons of Mealworms

The main pro of using mealworms as your gecko's main source of prey is the fact that they are not very active, they are unable to jump or climb, which means that there is virtually no chance of them escaping. A further benefit of using mealworms is the fact that they can be refrigerated for weeks on end which means that you do not need to worry about feeding and looking after your geckos prey. It is common practice to server mealworms to your leopard gecko in a small tray which simultaneously eliminates any chance of the worms ingesting the geckos fecal matter. The tray likewise makes it possible to provide your gecko with a tray of worms on a weekly basis simplifying the feeding process. However there are some negatives of using mealworms. Firstly, as previously mentioned, they are of less nutritional value than crickets and a far less stimulating prey for your gecko. It is possible to increase mealworms activity by introducing a small piece of vegetable to the tray that you place the meal worms in. The introduction of a vegetable allows the mealworms to move around and feed which will help to create a stimulating feeding process for your gecko. Similarly the exoskeleton of mealworms is potentially harder to digest than the exoskeleton of crickets.

Are Mealworms Dangerous for Geckos?

It is not uncommon for people to believe that mealworms are an unsuitable food source for leopard geckos as they believe that there is a possibility that a mealworm will eat its way out of the gecko's stomach lining. However there is absolutely NO validity to this belief. This misinformed belief has led many gecko owners to pinch the heads off of the mealworms before feeding them to their geckos. This is problematic as a leopard gecko will only eat live prey. Mealworms should always be served to your gecko alive. As previously mentioned mealworms have multiple benefits as a food source for your gecko and this myth should not deter you using mealworms as a primary prey source.

Gut Loading

The process of 'gut loading' involves feeding your prey of choice before feeding them to your gecko. The purpose of gut loading is to increase the nutritional value of the prey by feeding them food high in nutrients to transfer the nutrient to your gecko once the prey has been eaten. It is common to feed both crickets and mealworms carrots, oranges, pears and other vegetables for the purpose of gut loading. If you are using mealworms as your prey of choice it is best practice to place your gut loading food in the tray with the worms when you introduce them into the vivarium. This will allow for the mealworms to always be gut loaded and there is a possibility that your gecko will ingest the gut loading food directly while it ingests the mealworms.

Dusting the Prey

It is possible to dust your prey of choice in powders that

contain important vitamins and nutrients. To dust your prey of choice effectively place the prey and the powder in either a small can or small bag and shake gently to coat the prey's body in the powder. It is important to shake gently as you do not wish to kill the prey as this would make the gecko disinterested in eating it. It is likewise important to make sure that the prey does not have copious amounts of dust on its body to avoid the chance of dust getting into your gecko's eyes which could lead to an infection.

Pinkies and Waxworms

Both pinkies and waxworms are high in calories and are therefore a great way to increase your gecko's weight. It is common for leopard geckos to lose a lot of weight during periods of sickness and it is common for female geckos to lose weight during the breeding process – primarily after they have laid their eggs. Both pinkies and waxworms should not be the main source of feeding for your gecko as it is possible for geckos to become obese which leads to multiple health problems.

How much do Geckos eat?

Juvenile geckos should be fed daily. Adults on the other hand can be fed every other day. The best way to calculate how much you should feed your gecko is as follows:

2 adequately sized insects X your geckos total length in inches

(e.g. a 3inch gecko should be fed 6 insects per feeding)

Watering

Leopard geckos live in dry environments in the wild but still require some water and humidity to survive. It is important to provide your leopard gecko with a stable shallow water dish to avoid the chance of the gecko drowning or creating spillage. It is best practice to place the water on the cooler side of the cage to avoid the water evaporating too quickly. It is a good idea to mist your gecko's vivarium once or twice a week, especially if the gecko is about to shed.

SHEDDING

Like all reptiles and amphibians, leopard geckos shed their skin. Leopard geckos will shed their entire skin in a single shedding process. Juvenile geckos will shed their skin much more frequently than adult geckos due to the fact that they are still growing and will need to shed their skin as they outgrow it.

How to tell if your Gecko is about to Shed

If your leopard gecko's coloring has suddenly become duller do not worry. The coloring of a leopard gecko that is preparing to shed will slowly become more dull until their skin turns a whitish color. Once their skin has turned a whitish color they should immediately start the shedding process. It is important to check that your gecko has shed the entirety of its skin after each shedding session. It is not uncommon for a gecko to not fully remove the skin around their toes which if left unshed can lead to constriction of blood flow to the toe – which eventually leads to the toe dying and falling off.

Is it normal for my Gecko to eat its shed skin?

Do not be alarmed if your gecko eats it's shed skin as this is perfectly normal. There are two key reasons that a leopard gecko will always eat its shed skin. Firstly in the wild the gecko will eat its own skin to avoid alerting any predators to its presence. Secondly the shedding process uses energy and by eating the shed skin the gecko replenishes its energy,

A Moist Shelter

A moist shelter should be provided during the shedding process as it provides a higher level of humidity which assists the gecko in the shedding process. A good example of a moist shelter is a tapware container lined with cypress mulch or peat moss to create the moisture. It is not uncommon for leopard geckos to prefer moist shelters even when they are not going through the shedding process. As previously mentioned misting your gecko's vivarium during the shedding process is also a fantastic way of helping your gecko to shed its skin.

BREEDING

Leopard geckos are relatively easy to breed. This is due to the fact that a single male can, and will, mate with multiple females. Breeders tend to group one male with three or four females to optimize the breeding process.

How to tell if a Female Gecko is Pregnant

Pregnancy in females can, usually, be detected be feeling along their abdomen. If there are small bumps on either side of the females abdomen chances are she is pregnant. If a laying box is provided pregnant females will tend to use it rather than laying their eggs in random places around the vivarium. A laying box can be made in a similar way to the previously mentioned moist shelter.

Eggs

Females will normally produce multiple clutches of eggs during breeding season. Once the eggs have been laid they should be removed from the vivarium and incubated in an even mixture of water and vermiculite. A plastic shoebox, or tapware tub, make decent incubators. The incubator should be heated to about 85 degrees Fahrenheit which will normally allow the eggs to hatch after around two months. A higher incubator temperature will increase the chance of more females hatching from eggs. It is important to note that newly born geckos will tend to not eat until they have completed their first shed. Likewise it is important to separate newly born geckos from their parents.

HIBERNATION

Hibernation is a natural part of most reptiles yearly cycles and leopard geckos are not an exception to this. However it does not appear necessary for pet leopard geckos to hibernate due to the constant availability of food. It is therefore possible to continue to heat your vivarium throughout the winter and your gecko will remain active and healthy.

How to Hibernate your Gecko

Sometimes it is important for you to hibernate your gecko. It is normally enough to just turn off your under tank heater for your gecko to start the hibernation process. During the hibernation process your gecko will eat less, drink less and be vastly less active. It is common for leopard geckos to remain in hibernation for up to three months without losing much weight due to the fat stores in tails and their metabolism decreasing dramatically during the hibernation process. You should attempt to feed your gecko occasionally during the hibernation process but remove any uneaten insects within a few hours after offering them to your gecko.

FINAL THOUGHTS

Thank you for purchasing our pet care manual on caring for a leopard gecko. We hope you have found the information both interesting and informative. We hope that this book has allowed you to make an informed choice on whether owning a leopard gecko suits you and if so we hope that the information will help you to provide the best quality care for your pet gecko.

We will be publishing multiple other pet care manuals on our author page on Kindle. If you have an interest in exotic and exciting pets then we highly suggest you check out our other work.

I am passionate about providing the best quality information to our customers. We would highly appreciate any feedback, or reviews, you could leave us on our Kindle page to allow us to help create the best possible pet care products available on the market.

Leopard Gecko Care

Printed in Great Britain
by Amazon